The Little Book of
Church Signs

D1737796

Publishing, LLC

Kansas City

The Little Book of Church Signs

08 09 10 11 12 WKT 10 9 8 7 6 5 4 3 2 1

ISBN-13: 978-0-7407-7237-5
ISBN-10: 0-7407-7237-6

Library of Congress Control Number: 2007934927

Illustrations by Kevin Brimmer

www.andrewsmcmeel.com

THE PLATYPUS
PROVES THAT GOD
HAS A SENSE
OF HUMOR.

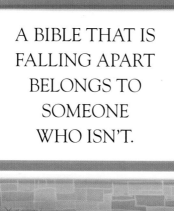

A BIBLE THAT IS
FALLING APART
BELONGS TO
SOMEONE
WHO ISN'T.

FIVE OUT OF FIVE
DENTISTS AGREE:
CHURCH IS GOOD
FOR YOUR SMILE.

Soul food
served here.

IF YOU WANT TO
HEAR GOD LAUGH,
TELL HIM
YOUR PLANS.

FRIENDS ARE
GOD'S WAY OF
APOLOGIZING TO US
FOR OUR FAMILIES.

ATHEISTS ARE
BEYOND BELIEF.

CARS AREN'T THE
ONLY THINGS
RECALLED
BY THEIR MAKER.

VISITORS
WELCOMED,
MEMBERS
EXPECTED.

NOTHING RUINS
THE TRUTH
LIKE STRETCHING IT.

PEOPLE WHO RELY
MOST ON GOD
RELY LEAST
ON THEMSELVES.

IMMEDIATE SEATING
AVAILABLE!

JESUS PAID A BILL
HE DIDN'T OWE.

THE PERSON WHO
SINGS HIS OWN
PRAISES IS PROBABLY
A SOLOIST.

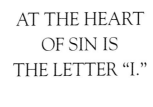

AT THE HEART
OF SIN IS
THE LETTER "I."

IN DEBT?
JESUS SAVES.

FORBIDDEN FRUIT
CREATES
MANY JAMS.

SOME THINGS
HAVE TO BE BELIEVED
TO BE SEEN.

BECOME
ANOTHER
DOPELESS HOPE
FIEND!

EVERYONE WANTS
TO GO TO HEAVEN,
BUT NO ONE
WANTS TO DIE.

DON'T MAKE ME
COME DOWN
THERE!

—GOD

GOD IS
THE POTTER,
WE ARE ONLY
HIS CLAY.

MAKE A FRIEND IN
HIGH PLACES.

THERE WILL NEVER
BE A REDUCTION
IN THE WAGES
OF SIN.

ENLIGHTEN UP!

EASTER IS MORE
THAN SOMETHING
TO DYE FOR.

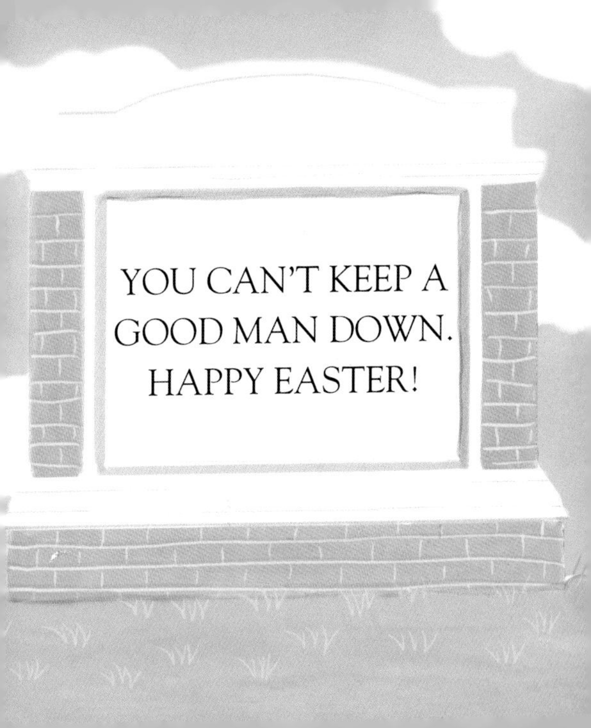
YOU CAN'T KEEP A
GOOD MAN DOWN.
HAPPY EASTER!

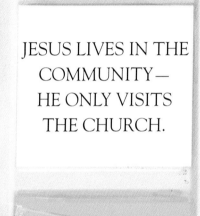

JESUS LIVES IN THE COMMUNITY—HE ONLY VISITS THE CHURCH.

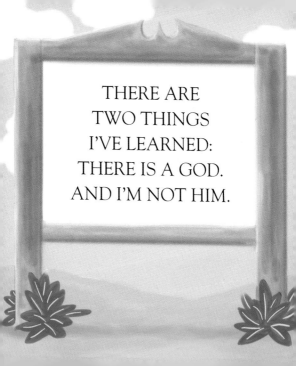

BLESSED ARE THE
FLEXIBLE, FOR
THEY SHALL NOT
BE BENT
OUT OF SHAPE.

LOST AND FOUND
INSIDE.

GOD LOVES US
THE WAY WE ARE,
BUT TOO MUCH
TO LET US
STAY THAT WAY.

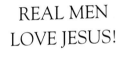

LIFE IS A PUZZLE.
LOOK HERE
FOR THE
MISSING PEACE.

PREPAID
MASTER'S CARD—
SIGN UP TODAY.

OUR
CONGREGATION
IS LIKE FUDGE.
MOSTLY SWEET,
WITH A FEW NUTS.

SIN:
THE ORIGINAL
SMOKE DETECTOR.

STACK EVERY BIT
OF CRITICISM
BETWEEN TWO
LAYERS OF PRAISE.

ALL OUR SEATS
COME WITH A
FIRST-CLASS SERVICE.

KEEP USING MY
NAME IN VAIN,
I'LL MAKE RUSH
HOUR LONGER.

—GOD

GIVE GOD
WHAT'S RIGHT,
NOT WHAT'S LEFT.

GOD DIDN'T
DO IT ALL
IN ONE DAY—
WHAT MAKES YOU
THINK YOU CAN?

SIN = SOUL IN NEED

JESUS INVESTED
HIS LIFE
IN YOURS—
HAVE YOU SHOWN
ANY INTEREST?

God's way
is the
high way.

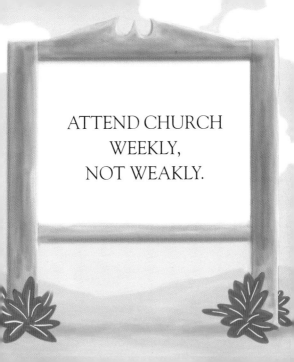

ATTEND CHURCH
WEEKLY,
NOT WEAKLY.

BLESSED ARE THOSE
WHO CAN LAUGH AT
THEMSELVES, FOR
THEY WILL NEVER
CEASE TO BE AMUSED.

COMMUNION
SUNDAY—
OVER A
BILLION SERVED.

You think
it's hot here?

SOULAR POWERED
BY THE SON.

JESUS CAN TURN
YOUR E-F-I-L
AROUND.

HOME IMPROVEMENT:
TAKE YOUR FAMILY
TO CHURCH.

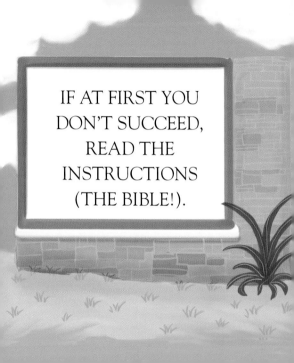

HELP IS JUST
A PRAYER AWAY.

COME WORK FOR THE LORD. THE WORK IS HARD, THE HOURS ARE LONG, AND THE PAY IS LOW. BUT THE RETIREMENT BENEFITS ARE OUT OF THIS WORLD.

PRAY UP
IN ADVANCE.

BIBLE:
BASIC
INSTRUCTIONS
BEFORE LEAVING
EARTH

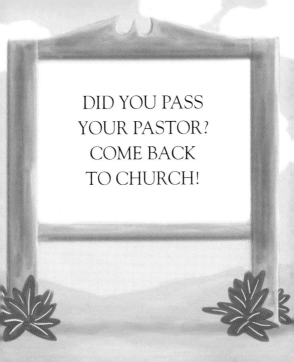

DID YOU PASS
YOUR PASTOR?
COME BACK
TO CHURCH!

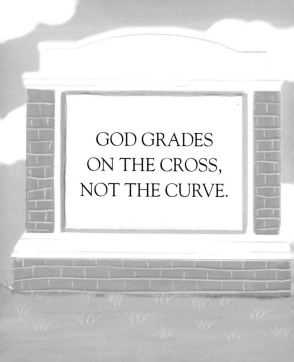

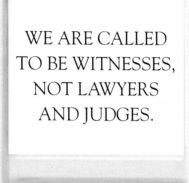

WE ARE CALLED
TO BE WITNESSES,
NOT LAWYERS
AND JUDGES.

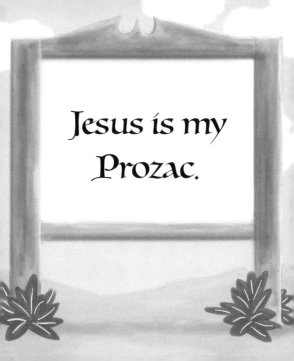

PRAYER IS THE KEY
OF THE DAY
AND THE LOCK
OF THE NIGHT.

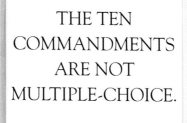

THE TEN
COMMANDMENTS
ARE NOT
MULTIPLE-CHOICE.

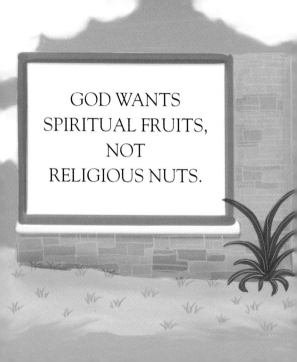

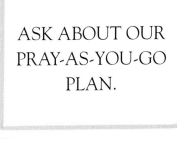

ASK ABOUT OUR
PRAY-AS-YOU-GO
PLAN.

Have a
God day!

STOP, DROP,
AND ROLL
DOES NOT WORK
IN HELL.

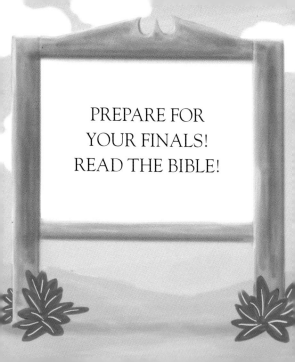

COUNT YOUR
BLESSINGS!
RECOUNTS
ARE OKAY.

EXERCISE DAILY—
WALK WITH
THE LORD.

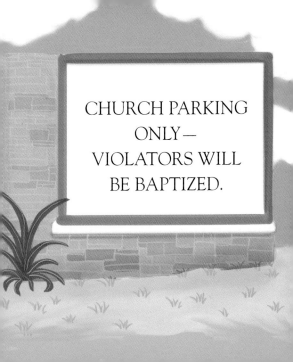

GOD IS.
ANY QUESTIONS?

A FAMILY ALTAR
CAN ALTER A FAMILY.

WHEN LIFE NEEDS
REBOOTING,
REMEMBER—
JESUS SAVES!

REDEMPTION
CENTER —
NO COUPON NEEDED.

RELIGION IS MEANT TO BE BREAD FOR DAILY USE, NOT CAKE FOR SPECIAL OCCASIONS.

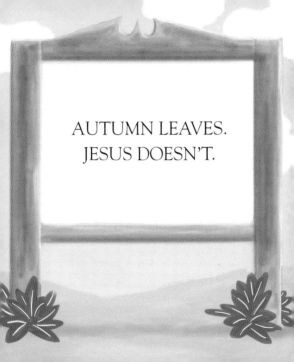

AUTUMN LEAVES.
JESUS DOESN'T.

GOD IS AT
THE END OF
YOUR ROPE.

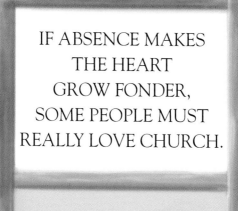

IF ABSENCE MAKES
THE HEART
GROW FONDER,
SOME PEOPLE MUST
REALLY LOVE CHURCH.

FREE WINE
EVERY SUNDAY!

WHAT THE
CHURCH NEEDS
IS LESS BLOCK
AND MORE TACKLE.

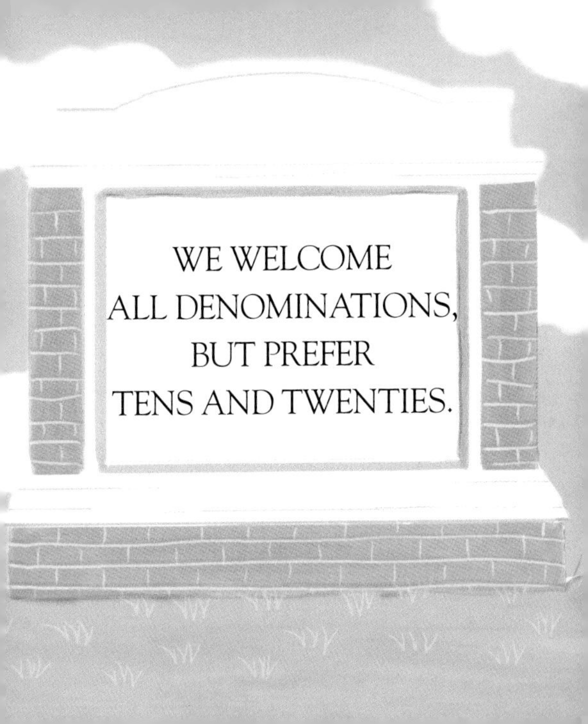
WE WELCOME
ALL DENOMINATIONS,
BUT PREFER
TENS AND TWENTIES.

SAME OWNER
FOR 2,000 YEARS.

BIG BANG THEORY:
GOD SPOKE AND
"BANG!"
IT HAPPENED.

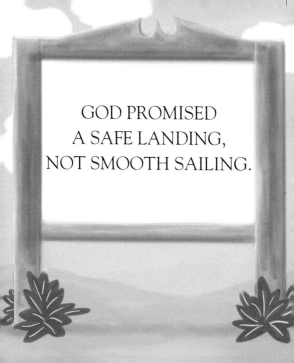

SOULED OUT!
KNEELING
ROOM ONLY.

SERVICE IS NOT
SERVE-US.

THOU SHALT
NOT LIE...
IN BED ON SUNDAY
MORNING!
COME TO CHURCH!

GOD WANTS
TO REIGN
ON YOUR PARADE!

AND YOU'RE
WORRIED ABOUT
SANTA'S
NAUGHTY-OR-NICE
LIST?

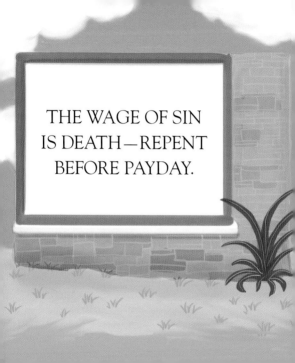

REMEMBER THE
REASON FOR
ALL SEASONS.

GOD BLESS US ALL!
NO EXCEPTIONS.

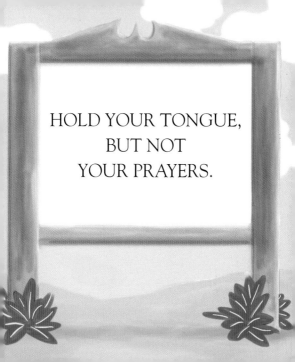

The end
is only
the beginning.